ON THE MINES

ON THE MINES

DAVID GOLDBLATT
NADINE GORDIMER

"This people, plunged wholly in the present,
lives with neither myths nor consolation."

Albert Camus

C. STRUIK (PTY) LTD

CAPE TOWN
1973

C. STRUIK (PTY) LTD

Africana Specialist and Publisher

First Edition

Copyright © 1973 David Goldblatt and Nadine Gordimer.

Credits

The quotation from Albert Camus' *Lyrical and Critical*,
translated by Philip Thody,
is made with the kind permission of the publishers,
Hamish Hamilton Ltd.

Grateful acknowledgement is made to the publishers of
Optima for their permission to reproduce photographs 28, 29, 30, 37 and 38 in this book.

ISBN O 86977 029 2

BOOK DESIGNED BY DAVID GOLDBLATT
LITHOGRAPHIC REPRODUCTIONS: MESSRS HIRT AND CARTER (PTY) LTD, CAPE TOWN
PRINTED BY: ABC PRESS (PTY) LIMITED, CAPE TOWN
BOUND BY PRINTPAK (CAPE) LTD, CAPE TOWN
PHOTOSET IN MONOPHOTO PLANTIN BY UNION PROCESS ENGRAVING & STEREO (PTY) LTD, CAPE TOWN

CONTENTS

ACKNOWLEDGEMENTS

Nadine Gordimer had a part in the making of my Witwatersrand photographs long before I met her. Her first book, Face to Face, *which I read in 1950, made explicit for me, to the point of pungency, my own then vague awareness of our milieu. And over the years, as I sought expression in photography, her writing came to be peculiarly relevant: challenging, affirming, always extending my understanding of what we both so often seemed to find significant.*

I started photographing the Witwatersrand in 1965 and by 1967 had done sufficient to feel that there was the possibility here of a worthwhile essay. In some trepidation I showed the photographs to Nadine Gordimer, with the suggestion that we might collaborate in exploring afresh our deep and abiding early impressions. To my delight she responded warmly, feeling that we shared a certain vision that, in my pictures and her words, might attain a new dimension for both. Charles Eglington, poet and literary critic, then editor of Optima, *commissioned the essay we envisaged and published it in 1968; it is now expanded in this book, to which, therefore, his enthusiasm as a sensitive and creative editor has also contributed.*

Through the help of Charles Eglington and Errol Fyfe, I photographed "sinking" for Optima *at Welkom in 1969. In 1970 I went underground again to complete the series which here forms the second essay.*

For their help and encouragement, I am grateful to Lionel Abrahams, Emil Brune, Alan and Marikje Bunton, Inez Cohen, Thelma Gutsche, Norman Hall, Sam and Alida Haskins, Barry Mortimer, David North, Allan Porter, Barney Simon, Olga, Nick, Lily, Steven, Brenda and Ron Goldblatt. I should also like to thank the many mining men who offered me kindly tolerance and sometimes very active assistance.

The photographs in this book owe much to my father, Eli Goldblatt, who never saw them. From his regard and love for the place in which we lived and its people, I learned.

D.G.

THE WITWATERSRAND:

a time and tailings

On nine farms in Africa in 1886 there began gold mining operations that were to produce great riches and political and economic power that would outlive the deposit of ore and the individual lives of successive generations of men who mined it. There also began a way of life shaped by the nature of the work to be done, the relationship of the strangers who came together to do it, and the blankness of the place on earth where they found themselves.

It had a name, of course: the highveld, part of the Transvaal, a rural republic; later the Union and then the Republic of South Africa. Names of farms became names of mines – simple designations, characterless as an X in place of a signature, identifying emptiness by its few natural features, a spring, a stream, a rise in the ground. Some Africans of the Ndebele and Sotho-Tswana peoples and about six hundred white farmers and their families had lived there; the farmers only seasonally, leaving the cold plateau for the lowveld, in the winters. Skirmishes between men, black and white, tribal wars, had blown across as the wind did. There were no monuments; no ruins.

The Witwatersrand created its own landscape out of waste and water brought from underground in the process of deep-level mining, and created its own style of living, inevitably following the social pattern of the colonial era of which it was a phenomenon, but driven by imperatives even deeper than the historical one. The social pattern was, literally and figuratively, on the surface; the human imperative, like the economic one, came from what went on below ground. Perhaps it always remained "below ground"; in men's minds, too. It belongs to the subconscious, from where what matters most in human affairs often never comes up to light, or does so disguised as coarse sentiment or expedience, patronage or indifference. Above, there were the neat standard houses and the recreation club of the white men, the compound and concession stores of the black men. The colour bar kept them separated. Below, at work, there was life-and-death dependency between them. It was codified in something called Safety Regulations. Such a code is the recognition of a final faith necessary between man and man, for survival.

The deep-level mines of the Witwatersrand, throwing up a trail of human habitation for more than sixty miles between Springs and Randfontein, never had about them the raffish atmosphere of the early diggers' camps and their mining village, Johannesburg. The day of the digger-adventurer ended there: the picks and shovels of nomads could not get at the Main Reef – only capital and technical resources had the right reach. The big mining companies put down upon the veld, men, machinery and money. Complete equipment for mining gold; raw materials for a settled human society. Cornish miners, and engineers, technicians, geologists and administrators with university degrees came from Britain and Europe. The eruption of gold through a static agricultural economy brought the sons of white farmers to the barracks of small rooms behind a wood-and-iron verandah – the Single Quarters built on "The Property" – and the uniform houses permanently darkened by wire-netting against flies – the Married Quarters. The pressures of a colonial money-economy brought young black men as migrant labour from tribes all over the country, and beyond, to the inward-facing Compounds on "The Property".

It was a company of strangers in a place without a past, with nothing to quiet that certain spiritual hunger whose bread is memory. This is a hunger common to men whether they have just emerged from an Iron Age, a semi-feudal agronomy, or are the educated products of modern capitalism. On the veld there were built the billiard-rooms of the General Manager's fretted wood-and-iron Residence, the squalid concrete bunks of the Compound. Both were thought apposite to needs – of whom? For what? A wood-and-iron version of the facilities of a Victorian country house party; a cross between a military barracks, a prison, and a boys' school. Within each, men put up a spider-web (tenacious, resilient) of a new personality, compounded of a tradition apparently impossible to share and a manner of dealing with the strange elements of the present.

In a curious way, the landscape came to express this just as it did the demands of the work that was being done. We who were born into it in the Twenties and Thirties opened our eyes not so much on God's creation as on our fathers' bold rearrangement of it. This was very different from the hedgerows and fields that domesticate the earth. This was a making of mountains and waters. There was even a smell to it all, a subterranean pollen-scent of chemicals, as of the minerals flowering underground. The forms were as austere as Egypt's; but these pyramids of tailings entombed no lost civilisation. It was ugly. Rusted iron, a three-day beard of prickly khaki-weed, the veld burned off and the sand blowing in the season that passes for spring, in Africa. But sometimes it became perversely, suddenly, the parody of picture-postcard beauty. The dust put a red filter over the suspended sun; the step-pyramids and cones were repeated, upside down, in the lakes of dead water. Where the water was shallow it shone mother-of-pearl in its impurity or left a brilliant verdigris on the sand. Every horizon bore the seal of a shaft-head, stamped black.

The style of the mines was a New Brutalism. Galvanised iron was its material. Confronted with one of the old steam hoists, or a vast pump all tentacles, to be housed, the mine draughtsman was driven to a solution by the purest principles of functional design. The building blocked out the space necessary for the efficient working of the machine, and its shape followed – of necessity abstracted into the sharp planes and angles natural to sheets of galvanised iron – the machine's contour: the *appearance* of a building came about. And it was no more than that: to read the meaning of these structures, you must go inside and see what piece of work is performed there.

There are quite a few left, on the properties which are being or about to be demolished. Galvanised iron – the stuff of makeshift – has lasted the lifetime of the Witwatersrand mines. Studded together like wings of an aircraft, curling loose here and there at the corners but holding – these facades whose texture, when they were new, came only from the stripe of light and shadow on their corrugations, are mossed with rust, tarnish, faded paint and dirt. Each sheet of iron weathers differently, as if they never really belonged together any more than they can be made out to once they are piled as scrap.

Where they still stand these tin halls hold the marvellous machines for which they were made. There is a steam-powered hoist, vast as a dinosaur skeleton, but still in the full, shiny, steel-black, coal-black flesh of use. You have to walk around it to take it in; it is inert; a bell rings signalling that the load of men or ore is ready to come up from the mine, and then, set in motion and controlled by hand, there slides into vigour the huge rhythm and counter-rhythm of richly-oiled cogs and bobbing, interlocking components, gnashing behind japanned guard-pieces as twirly and a thousand times as grand as an old Singer.

Lugged and rocked across seas and veld from Europe fifty or sixty years ago, the machine age was unloaded on a place that had missed it out, like so much else. The machines were of a time when power was manifest in the mechanistic equivalent of a man's sweating and grunting in labour; the steam hoist, at only one remove from the effort of muscle, is controlled by fist and judgment of the winding-engine driver, who sits above it all in a wooden cabin or a chair home-made in the mine carpenters' shop. His face has the coarse-grained pallor and alertness of men who work with machines stronger than themselves and more deafening than men's voices. He is perhaps the last of his line; the last on whose steadiness of grip on a lever could depend the lives of a cage full of men hung in the depths of the earth. High upon the winding gear that guides a steel cable thick as Rapunzel's hair out near the roof to the shaft headgear and thence underground, and receives another threaded in from the opposite end of the process, a second man climbs about. Single light-bulbs like drops of yellow oil float on the dimness; his bare black legs take a shine. As the cable plays out past a measure on which the levels are shown, he daubs it with white paint to mark the point at which, on the return journey from the earth, it must be stopped. The cable comes up, the driver brings the hoist to a standstill with its great dragon's sigh, the man is busy wiping paint off as he has done an uncountable number of times.

When this mine closes, as it will soon, the men may continue their working lives in the new mines of the Far West or the Orange Free State. But now electric power is unseen and unheard – perhaps a faint hum, hardly more than the sound of one's blood in one's ears. The steam-powered hoist will be scrap at R20 a ton. Yet these were the real beauties, on the Property: the great machines, the huge, hell's oven boilers, the bright locomotives with their policeman's helmet cowls and gilt-on-green decorative scrolls. Theirs was an aesthetic expressing the reality of the place, the work, the daily human experience. It was to be found; but not in the chemically-coloured reflections of sunsets.

Between two and three hundred thousand black men a year have worked the mines of the Witwatersrand. They always far outnumbered the twenty to forty-two thousand white miners, technicians, and administrators. They came from Tanzania, Rhodesia, Mozambique, Malawi, Swaziland, Lesotho, Botswana – almost everywhere south of the Sahara – as well as the Transkei and Zululand. Migratory labour: the official term takes its metaphor from birds in their seasonal exodus in search of the means of life. But in South Africa it is also used of men who seek the means of life within their own country yet whose right to settle and bring their families to the region where they work is not recognised. The men have come and gone over more than half a century. They left behind them their great part in the complex of men and machinery whose momentum has powered the most diversified industrial state on the African continent. They took away a pittance in money and possessions. The things that black miners coveted, the gramophones, flower-papered trunks, watches and cheap suits were the least of it; what the experience has meant to them is difficult to trace, since most are not literate, and they speak with a variety of Africa's seven hundred tongues.

The black man came to the mines to earn bride-price and taxes and acquired new skills as he did so. As for his social and spiritual needs, in some tribes, in territories far distant from the Witwatersrand, the six- to twenty-month spell of labour in the gold mines became one of the trials attesting to the attainment of full adulthood. Once back from the mines, you are a man. Most white people accept this as the sum of the experience for black miners.

Emancipated blacks and both black and white spokesmen for the African personality see the black man's experience of the mines as a traumatic one. Labour underground epitomises the black man's baptism by darkness and dust into Western civilisation. Tribesman comes to Jo'burg – the obsessive theme of African writing from Vilikazi's poem IN THE MINES to Peter Abraham's MINE BOY – is the twentieth century myth of Africa, gathering to itself round one simple story all the harsh and bewildering experience of a forced rebirth from one age to the unknown of another.

Which interpretation comes nearest the reality? One thing is certain. Man comes naked into the world again when he is industrialised. The price is higher than bride-price. And if those in command of the process are white and he is black and seen as a unit of labour rather than a man, rags and shoddy are what he will get for a long, long time. The wage-gap between black and white mine-workers was twelve to one in 1911. It had increased to more than twenty to one by 1969. It was not until 1973 that the miners' trade unions, whose membership continues, by law, to be confined to whites, agreed that certain strictly limited categories of skilled jobs would be opened to black miners. Black wages have been raised; white artisans have had to be "compensated" for this concession of white privilege by "responsibility" allowances. The gap between white earnings and black has come nowhere near being closed. The mining industry was the basis of South Africa's industrial wealth and long ago set the pattern for the exploitation of blacks by whites. Much has changed; not this. Weighed against gold, the white man's sweat is still considered of greater worth than the black man's.

Early on Sunday mornings, not many hours after the dance band had played "Goodnight Sweetheart" to the whites in the Recreation Hall, the drums began to sound for the dancing at the Compound, on the properties of the Witwatersrand. Not only the people of The Property, but the whole population of the mining towns woke to the beat of drums; it was as unremarkable to us as church bells. Into the new rhythm of working by shift down the mine instead of by season on the land, the black miners brought the familiar rhythms of tribal dances. The dances lacked the context of occasion that belonged to them, at home. They became adapted to, expressive of the new situation, just as the traditional seed-pod rattles worn round the dancers' ankles became bottle-caps. Among the stock-in-trade characters of the dancing mimes, the white Shift Boss appeared. Few white people were aware of their image, integrated into the black man's new world: yet it was there to be seen, in the things that made us smile or that we found incomprehensible – the trousers tied with string beneath the knee, for example, which were not recognized as representing the high boots worn by the heroes of the Westerns shown at Compound cinema shows, and the busy arrangement of the paraphenalia of watches, badges, cline rules, pens and pencils worn by Boss Boys, caricature and apotheosis of white red tape. Sometimes a white miner would bring one of his gang of "boys" home to his house on the Property to perform some odd job. I remember going with a small friend, who had been detailed to take one of these men a mug of tea: we two children, carefully carrying it across the garden to where the black man was helping to lay a brick path. "Go on, take it," my friend's father said. The black man stood up and wiped his hands on his trousers; in the light of day, above ground, the two men smiled at the children. "That's my son" said the white man; it was a kind of hospitality. But the black miner could only smile. The two men could communicate only in the patois of work. Their relationship was defined in phrases from the MINER'S COMPANION – IN ENGLISH, AFRIKAANS, SESUTO AND MINE KAFFIR: *Come here.*

Go there. What is your name? To what tribe do you belong? Do you understand mines? I don't want a loafer. I cannot afford to feed and pay loafers.

The white people on the mines of the Witwatersrand began their life together lost in many kinds of isolation; yet, speaking of the past, anyone who lived there will give the strongest impression of security. Mining people not only worked together; they lived close in Company houses along Company streets, tended by a mine doctor in the mine hospital, meeting at the mine Recreation Club for their entertainment, playing tennis and soccer on the mine's courts and fields with the mine teams. One could go from christening to old age pension within the shelter of the Company plantations of blue gums that surrounded The Property. One need never be aware of the threatening space of the veld without. Inside the magic circle of blue gums everything was decided for one, from annual leave to social status; a cosy society, with every draughty gap where loneliness might blow in stopped by the immediate availability of a talk over the fence or a game of billiards down at the Rec, where all faces were as familiar as one's wife's. *We were just like one big family in those days.* What other way could there have been of making a community in that emptiness, that memoryless place? It was an autocratic family, of course, and the social hierarchy, based on the hierarchy of working importance, provided the sense of order. The General Manager's in his residence; all's well with the world. Like all family systems, this one exacted unquestioning conformation, admitted no possibilities of doubt about its mores, gave little access to the world of ideas; and offered in return a sense of belonging whose time, like that of the mines themselves, has now run out.

There is still more than half as much known gold in the ground of South Africa as has been taken out of it since 1886. Most of it is in the new mines, under the dusty Brasilias of the Far West and the Free State. Some of it is still in the rock of the mines of the Witwatersrand; in the mountains of waste; swept into the very crevices of the old buildings on the Properties; even in the dust that grits between your teeth as you follow the Main Reef Road East to West. A deposit of ore is finite; and so people talk of the "dying" mines as if these were living organisms with a natural span. But a mine does not last as long as the veins of ore last, as a man lives while he has blood flowing in his veins. Somewhere the word is pronounced: "Given an unchanged gold price and the present rate of erosion of values, the Chamber calculates that R2 000 million worth of gold will have to be abandoned." A mine lives only so long as the percentage of gold recovered from it is payable in relation to the price of gold and the great, spangled juggling act of the country's economy. All along the Witwatersrand now, the bulldozers advance, the winches stop turning. Those single unshaded light bulbs which burned everywhere in the prodigality of "mine" electricity, making the mine's own daylight in sheds and offices and fly-screened Quarters of the Property, go out – following economic decrees as apparently immutable as natural laws. The towns that grew up like camp followers to live off the spending of the mining communities are taking The Properties into urban anonymity without a trace. Here a Recreation Club has been bought and painted a fashionable pink by a local immigrant community, for their Sunday gatherings – the false gable above the verandah lettered ΕΛΛΗΝΙΚΟΣ ΣΥΝΔΕΣΜΟΣ ΣΠΡΙΝΓΚΣ A mine golf course is taken over by a municipality. An engineering firm moves into the old Time offices, with their pergola of dead roses and empty fishpond, where in the gaunt presence of the shafthead and the sizzling of the cooling system nearby, some Time Officer saw to it that a gang of "boys" kept the place "nice".

The landscape that was made is being dismantled. A composite of men and machinery that industrialized a white rural community and tens of thousands of tribal black people is being disengaged. Once, long ago, white-tailed Gnu, Blesbok, Springbok, Hartebeest, Eland and Quagga roamed there. There was no one to remember. Once, not long ago, these Properties were strongly-characterized human units, homogeneous in their labour and in the solutions they found to their needs, whether these were fulfilled by amateur barbers among the black miners, setting up soap-box, scissors and mirror under the Compound pepper trees, or by members of the white Christmas Party Committee, considering wholesalers' lists of toys. Everyone is forgetting fast. The money, technological advance and economic power the Witwatersrand mines brought up from the darkness flows into human activities removed from them in nature and time. The children and grandchildren of the black miners who came from neighbouring territories are the M.P.s and executives as well as the clerks and labourers of independent black states. The children and grandchildren of South African black miners provide for secondary industry at home, as they did for the mines, the overwhelming majority of the labour force in exchange for the smallest share of the returns. The children and grandchildren of the white miners sell real estate, run businesses and industries, work in factories, and live in industrial towns which bear the names of those farms on which the auriferous conglomerates were found. All are faces among faces, interchangeable as those of city dwellers everywhere, recognizing no familial likeness of dependency.

The shaftheads are the totem objects of the extinct frontier society. There are no ghosts where the price of ground is measured per square foot. Already the model township covers the General Manager's garden and the Compound, giant shadows prance on the screen of the drive-in cinema built on a mine dump. Everywhere the mountains of past endeavour are being grassed over, like so many suburban parks.

Nadine Gordimer

3
Winder house.
Farrar Shaft, Angelo, 1965

1
Ore train and amputated headgear.
Geduld, Springs, July 1965

2
Waste rock dump.
Randfontein Estates, May 1967

4

*Stripped headgear.
Comet Deep, East Rand Proprietary Mines,
November 1965*

Tailings wheel and mill foundations.
Wit. Deep, August 1966

6

Disused steam hoist.
Ferguson, Randfontein Estates,
March 1966

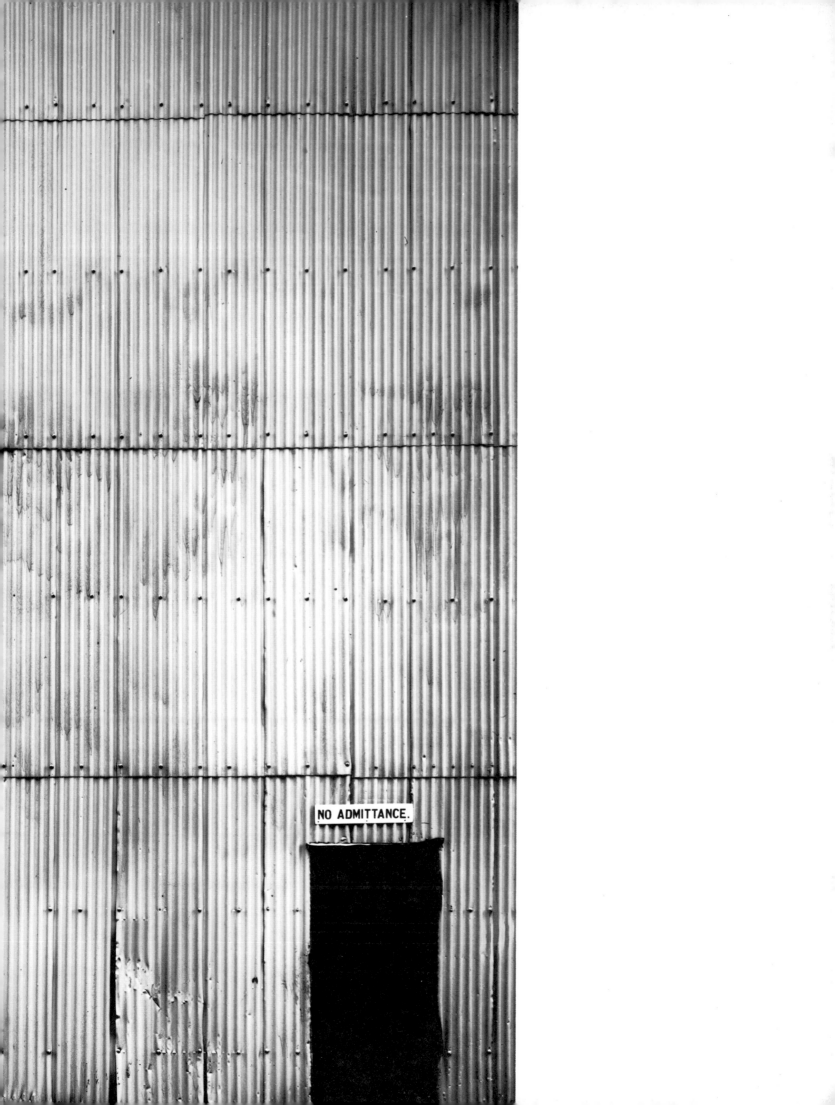

NO ADMITTANCE.

9

Poster for the prevention of accidents.
Central Salvage Yard, Randfontein Estates,
November 1966

7

Winder house wall.
No. 3 North, Randfontein Estates,
November 1965

8

Concession store.
Knights, 1965

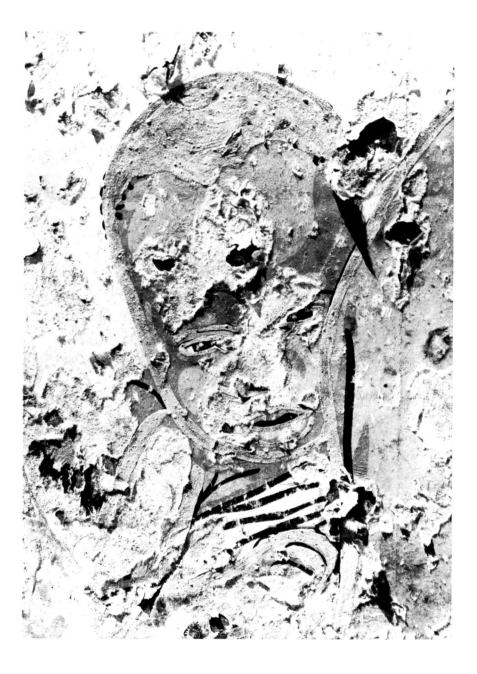

Concession store interior.
Crown Mines, Johannesburg,
May 1967

Barber's chair of mining timbers.
Luipaardsvlei Estate, Krugersdorp, 1965

12

"Boss Boy".
Battery Reef, Randfontein Estates, 1966
In right pocket:
clinometer for underground measurements,
notebook for recording them,
pens and pipe.
On left arm: company rank badge.
Three stars indicate that he is a Mine Overseer's Boss Boy.
On wrists: plastic identity band, ornamental
copper and rubber bands.
On belt: pocket knife in homemade sheath and Zobo watch
presented by the company
in recognition of accident-free work.

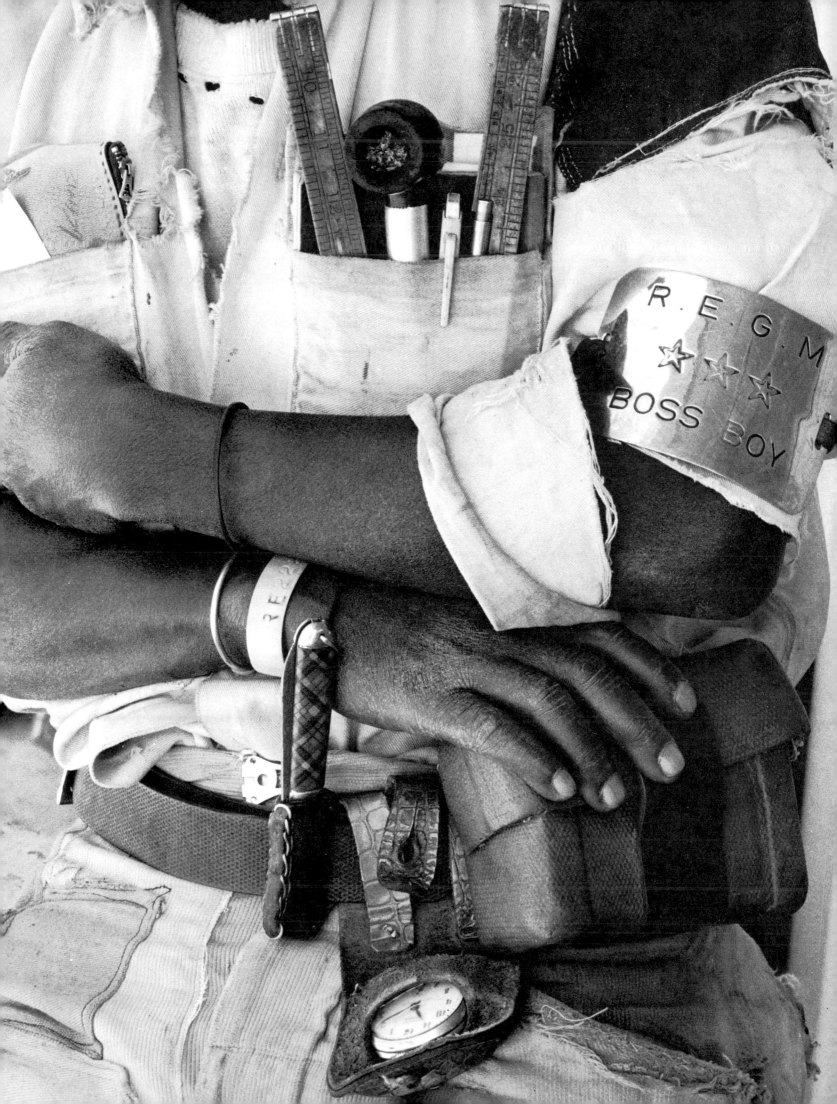

*Call system used by officials at a mine office
when they wanted the services of the African messenger.
Consolidated Main Reef Mine,
October 1967*

14

African mineworker's bunk with pin-ups.
Demolished compound near Springs,
July 1965

15

Poster for the prevention of accidents.
Central Salvage Yard, Randfontein Estates,
November 1966

Mine church.
Robinson, Randfontein Estates,
February 1966

Former head office of a mining house:
The Corner House, Johannesburg,
May 1965

"Dirty" bath and "clean" bath
for use of the General Manager after he came
up from underground.
Mine offices, New Kleinfontein, Benoni,
May 1967

19

Banksman's chair.
No. 3 North,
Randfontein Estates,
1965

*Model village built in the 1930's by African
mineworkers at their compound.
Brakpan Mine,
August 1966*

Coat of arms on the mine clubhouse.
Brakpan, 1967

General Manager's house.
Croesus, 1966

Bowling club.
Crown Mines, Johannesburg,
1969

General Manager's house.
New Kleinfontein, Benoni,
November 1965

Miner's cottage and slimes dump.
Near New Modder, Benoni,
August 1965

26

Building windbreaks
preparatory to planting grass on a mine dump.
Crown Mines, Johannesburg,
November 1965

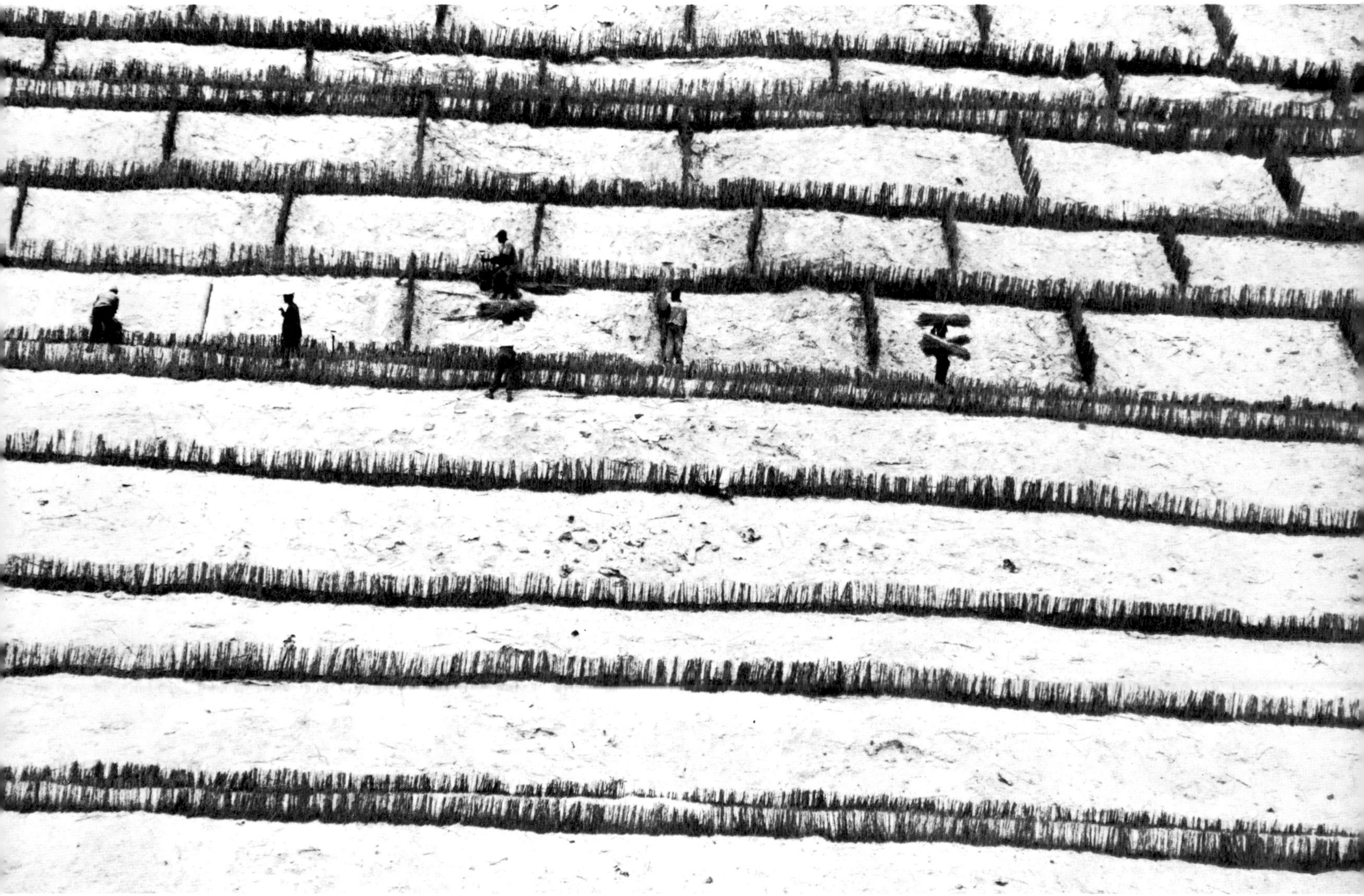

27

Shovels.
Central Salvage Yard, Randfontein Estates,
1966

SHAFTSINKING

Water rains ceaselessly onto the shaft bottom which consists of jagged heaps of loose rock flung up by the previous blast. Fifty feet above is the only illumination: four lamps fixed to the underside of the stage. The stage hangs, six stories and eighty tons of steel, on ropes from the surface. As the shaft deepens, so the stage will be lowered further. On it work the men who line the shaft with concrete and fit it out for the gold mine it is to serve.

Here on the bottom are the shaftsinkers. Up to seventy-two Basuto with a white Sinker and Sinker's Helper, who drill and blast and dig for upward of three years to gouge this hole eight or nine thousand feet vertically into the earth's crust. They generally word from "blast to blast". This should mean three eight-hour shifts per day. But often it needs more than eight hours to clear the bottom of rock and charge up for the next round. Sometimes a team will work for fourteen hours in furious assault upon the rock, not leaving the shaft bottom. And but for a few remarkable moments of tranquillity between one phase of work and the next, there is no respite.

The first task is to clear the bottom as quickly as possible of the rock loosened by the previous blast. From the underside of the stage hangs a great mechanical jaw at the end of an articulated arm: the cactus grab. This sweeps down and around the bottom, taking up mouthsful of rock and dumping them into great buckets or kibbles. Fourteen tons of rock per kibble and if there are no delays, about sixty-two kibbles per shift. In the thirty-three feet diameter circle of the shaft, the men jump and slither over the rock heaps, either dodging the comings and goings of kibbles and cactus or assisting in their digestion of rock. Every now and then there is total darkness as the lights go on and off: visual signalling where bells would not be heard in the deafening shriek of machinery and of metal on rock.

A kibble comes down through holes cut out for it in the stage above, looming over the bottom. Five or six men rush at it, shoulders phalanxed. They reach its side at precisely the moment before the bucket touches bottom, so that their momentum carries its base to the more or less even ground they have selected for it. As it settles, four men swarm up its sides to unhitch the hoist cable. A full kibble will then be hauled up while the first is loaded. The men jump down – a good ten feet – and pick themselves up, laughing and jubilant like boys on boulders. Basuto are said to be the best in the world at this work. They will tolerate no other tribesmen in their teams.

After the large rocks have been lifted out, the smaller stuff is hand-shovelled into a kibble. And when all the rubble has been cleared, the floor is blown over with air at high pressure, to expose misfires from the previous blast. The atmosphere becomes charged with grit and water driven at gale force. Except behind the blade of a shovel, there is no shelter from the cutting blast. From the awful scream of compressed air, there is no escape whatever.

Then suddenly it is over: the bottom is clean and incredibly there is no noise.

Light filters gently through the settling haze. The men, in oilers and gumboots, stand ungainly, at rest. Soon, from the surface, come pneumatic drills and intestine-like loops of heavy rubber hose. To each drill a water and an air hose are connected. "Machine men" take up drills, some, as though in obscene rite, sit with the hoses coiled between their legs. Drilling starts. Thirty-six drills and "total" noise, wholly enclosing and penetrating the head. Water, to dampen the deadly dust raised by the drills, fogs the atmosphere so that all is clothed, incongruously, in soft mist. When two-hundred-and-thirty-eight holes in a precisely determined pattern have been bored into the rock, the drilling stops. Now the equipment is hauled out, explosives are lowered and each hole is charged up and electrically connected. The sinking crew are pulled up, the stage is raised some two-hundred-and-fifty feet out of harm's way and the stage crew are evacuated. Then the blast is detonated from the surface.

Hanging over the shafthead in kibbles, the fresh team are already waiting for the fumes to clear the bottom before plunging downward to begin the new shift.

There are many variations of and diversions from this work pattern. Underground water is intersected, so long holes must be drilled ahead of the shaft and cement grout pumped like toothpaste into them until it closes all the fissures and staunches the flow. The bottom may flood and have to be pumped out. Sometimes, the kibbles lift not rock, but water; twenty tons at a time. There are treacherous rock strata that crumble and slide before the retaining concrete of the shaft lining can be poured. And there is methane gas. A good deal of the work on a shaft is involved with maintenance of equipment, repair of breakdowns and the prevention of accidents. The surprising feature about accidents in shaftsinking, is that they are not more frequent.

In the confines of that hole, men use great force to tear into the unyielding but not inert mass of rock. They are not remote from the point of confrontation. They are in it. Indeed they are of it. Some are maimed and killed. Rock from the sidewall slips; kibbles topple over; steel snaps; men forget and machines kill.

While charging up at the bottom there is some terrible concatenation of events and fifty-seven men are obliterated by explosives at Buffelsfontein Gold Mine in 1969. How frail and vulnerable men seem down there. Can there be truth in the shaftsinkers' boast that they feel safer on the bottom than when driving on the road?

The safety of the men and the shaft (for even a shaft can be 'lost') and the progress of the whole operation, is the direct responsibility of one man: the Master Sinker. Fabled as a hard-drinking tough guy, he needs, aside from a clear head and considerable know-how, an intuitive ability to make right decisions on the spot, often under difficult conditions. Not only are lives, pay packets and huge capital directly dependent on his ability, but over the longer term, the willingness of his men to follow him in unstinting obsession with the shaft.

All men employed on the shaft participate in bonuses based on footage sunk. The sooner the shaft is completed, the sooner can mining proper – and profits – begin. So there is strong inducement to work hard. But the men on a 'good' shaft are possessed by their work. Their commitment goes beyond the pay packet. Shaft-sinkers say that theirs is a man's job, that they could not stand the dull routine of ordinary mining. Miners say that shaftsinkers are mad.

To thrust so hugely and deeply and yet so precisely into the density and blackness of the earth is surely an act of supreme audacity.

David Goldblatt

The above description of shaftsinking is based on what I saw at President Steyn No. 4 Shaft, Welkom in 1969 and 1970. The photographs were made there at depths between 1 200 and 5 000 feet – except the picture (No. 31), which was taken at South Vaal in 1968.—D.G.

Going down in the kibble, daylight disappearing above,
pipes on the shaft-lining streaking past

While the stage is being lowered to a new position,
the shaftsinking team cluster below in the centre
of the shaft bottom.
There they should escape
any rock dislodged from the sidewall
by the movement of the stage

The sidewall :
treacherous shale at this stage.
As the shaft deepens,
so the stage will be lowered and its crew will line
the sidewall with concrete

*A kibble loaded with rock
has just been shackled to the hoist cable.
Above is the stage and under it at left,
is the grab cabin*

Underground water has been intersected.
Long drills are boring "cover" holes
into which cement will be pumped to staunch the flow.
A crew hoists a drill,
while on a kind of trapeze in the background,
a machine man drills

*Air and water hoses being connected
for drilling the blast holes*

Drilling begins :
238 holes

Machine men
fogged in dust-damping water

Sheltering behind a shovel
while the bottom is blown over
to uncover misfires

"Lashing"
or loading a kibble

Looking up the shaft at a kibble
about to pass through the stage

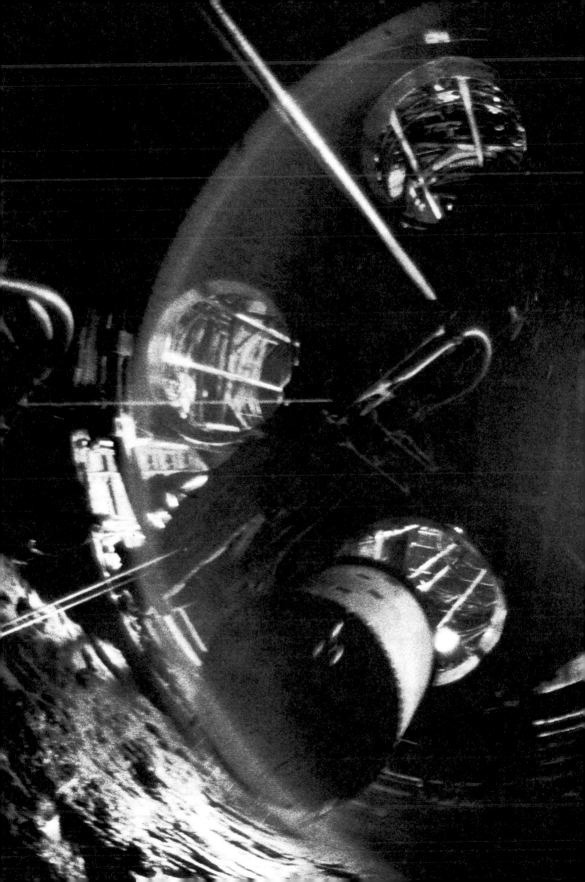

MINING MEN

Basuto shaftsinkers seeking work.
President Steyn No. 4, Welkom,
1969

40

B. Falk, mine captain.
City Deep, Johannesburg,
1966

Time Office Clerks.
City Deep, Johannesburg,
1966

Concession store proprietor (front) and assistant.
Rose Deep, Germiston,
October 1966

43

Joe Maloney,
Boiler House Attendant.
City Deep, Johannesburg,
1966

Nurse,
mine hospital.
Consolidated Main Reef Mines, Roodepoort,
October 1966

Greaser.
No. 2 North winder,
Randfontein Estates,
1965

46

Gang on surface work.
Rustenburg Platinum Mine,
1971

47

Chief Draughtsman and Sampler.
Mine offices, Consolidated Main Reef Mines, Roodepoort,
September 1967

48

Pondo mineworkers in their compound.
Carletonville,
1970

Masotho shaftsinking Machine Man.
President Steyn No. 4, Welkom,
1969

50

*Spanner Man.
Carletonville,
1970*

51

Butch Britz, Master Sinker.
President Steyn No. 4, Welkom,
1969

Miner.
Consolidated Main Reef Mines, Roodepoort,
1967

Harry Oppenheimer,
mining house chairman.
Johannesburg,
1966

54

*Sinker's Helper.
President Steyn No. 4, Welkom,
1969*

Basuto mineworkers in their compound.
Carletonville,
1970

56

Shiftboss and Lashing Men in a stope.
Consolidated Main Reef Mines, Roodepoort,
1967